T0348312

PLATFORM PAPERS

QUARTERLY ESSAYS ON THE PERFORMING ARTS

No. 16
April 2008

CURRENCY HOUSE

PLATFORM PAPERS
Quarterly essays from Currency House Inc.

Editor: Dr John Golder, j.golder@unsw.edu.au

Currency House Inc. is a non-profit association and resource centre advocating the role of the performing arts in public life by research, debate and publication.

Postal address: PO Box 2270, Strawberry Hills, NSW 2012, Australia

Email: info@currencyhouse.org.au   Tel: (02) 9319 4953
Website: www.currencyhouse.org.au   Fax: (02) 9319 3649

Editorial Board: Katharine Brisbane AM, Dr John Golder, John McCallum, Greig Tillotson

The Permanent Underground: Australian Contemporary Jazz in the New Millennium copyright © Peter Rechniewski, 2008

Except as permitted under the *Copyright Act* 1968, no part of this book may be reproduced without written permission. For details of the Copyright Agency Ltd licence, under the Act, for educational institutions, please contact CAL at info@copyright.com.au.

ISBN 978-0-9802802-6-5
ISSN 1449-583X

Typeset in 10.5 Arrus BT
Printed by Hyde Park Press, Adelaide

This edition of Platform Papers is supported by the Keir Foundation, the Greatorex Foundation and individual donors. To them and to all our supporters Currency House extends sincere gratitude.

Currency House's touring program is proudly sponsored by the Copyright Agency Limited.

Contents

AVAILABILITY *Platform Papers*, quarterly essays on the performing
arts, is published every January, April, July and October and is
available through bookshops or by subscription. For order form,
see page 72.

LETTERS Currency House invites readers to submit letters of
400–1,000 words in response to the essays. Letters should be
emailed to the Editor at info@currencyhouse.org.au or posted to
Currency House at PO Box 2270, Strawberry Hills, NSW 2012,
Australia. To be considered for the next issue, the letters must be
received by 15 May 2008.

CURRENCY HOUSE For membership details, see our website at:
www.currencyhouse.org.au

The Permanent Underground

Australian Contemporary Jazz in the New Millennium

PETER RECHNIEWSKI

The author

Peter Rechniewski first encountered live jazz when, as schoolboys, he and a friend wandered into El Rocco Jazz Cellar in 1967 and heard the John Sangster Quintet. He studied Arts at the University of Sydney, majoring in Medieval History and later did postgraduate studies at the University of New England and the University of New South Wales.

After several periods spent living in England, where he heard many of the great jazz musicians, he returned to Australia in 1982, slowly becoming involved in the jazz scene through the committee of the Jazz Action Society. Along with a number of fellow jazz enthusiasts, in 1984 he co-founded the Sydney Improvised Music Association (SIMA), of which he continues to be president and artistic director. He also served for many years as a committee member and vice-president of the Jazz Co-ordination Association of New South Wales. For five years he wrote a jazz column for a now defunct street paper and presented a jazz radio program on 2MBS–FM. He continues to teach in the NSW Public Education System.

Author's acknowledgements

I would like to thank those people who have contributed directly to this essay by responding to my questionnaire: Jim Budd, Louise Denson, Dan Quigley, Ingrid James, Lynette Irwin, Alan Corbet, Gary Lee, Dr Sylvan Elhay; Martin and Adrian Jackson for submitting to interviews and providing information along the way; Kate Lidbetter and Vanessa Chalker of the Music Board, Australia Council, Victoria Owens of Arts NSW; Dr Richard Letts of the Music Council of Australia; Mal Stanley and Gerry Koster of ABC Classic FM and Miriam Thompson for her valuable research in the archives of John Fairfax. Thanks also to my friend and SIMA co-founder Peter Jordan for many helpful suggestions and to Dr Elizabeth Rechniewski for her support and advice. Special thanks must go to Katharine Brisbane and John Golder of Currency House for caring enough about the state of Australian jazz to commission this paper. Finally, I'd like to thank all those jazz musicians whose playing has inspired, and occasionally consoled, me over so many years.

1

Oh, it's a jazz story

In August 2003, Jamie Oehlers, a young Australian musician based in Melbourne, landed in Sydney to play at the Side On Café, then the city's main contemporary jazz venue. Oehlers, a tenor saxophonist, performed with a local rhythm section before an enthusiastic crowd and flew home the following day. Another gig, another few dollars and satisfied fans. The performance wasn't reviewed, but perhaps it stayed in the memories of those who heard it and the local musicians who performed it. It would have taken a very observant reader to notice a tiny item in the same day's *Sydney Morning Herald*, telling us that Oehlers had just won the White Foundation World Saxophone Competition at Montreux, Switzerland, held during the Montreux Jazz Festival. In Melbourne, the *Age* also felt the event deserved similar coverage.

Such an achievement might have been thought worthy of at least a small feature, perhaps with a photograph. Indeed, if arts editors had shown a little more curiosity, they would have discovered something even more significant about the 2003 competition—one that sign-posted important developments in the Australian jazz scene itself.

Jamie Oehlers had come second in the same competition the previous year. Winning showed that he was not only talented, but also determined. Going against the trend of pop culture trivia and celebrity gossip that often passes for arts news in the Australian press, here was an opportunity to run something substantial, a deserving story about talent and determination finally winning out. But there was more to the story: not only had one Australian won, but another, Willow Neilson, had come third, while yet another, David Rex, had been placed among the twelve finalists.

I can find no evidence of any other international music competition in which Australians have made up a quarter of the finalists, let alone provided two of the three place-getters, including the winner. There was a modest feature in the *Australian* and in Oehlers' birth city of Perth, the *West Australian* also ran a piece.[1] The occasion should have been celebrated, not only on the arts pages of our newspapers, but also on ABC arts programs, and on *The 7.30 Report*. It should have been, but it wasn't—because the art form was jazz, the music you can dismiss or ignore if, as an editor or executive producer, you are short of space, reporters, time or money, or if you simply don't like jazz.

Of course, the Australian triumph at Montreux in 2003 could be seen as a mere coincidence that said little about the state of contemporary jazz in Australia, a matter of three talented musicians being in the same place at the same time, playing their best and impressing the judges. However, the media silence makes one wonder about the range of interests of most of the arts-reporting community. Had anyone been interested, they could have determined, without much effort, that a new wave of creativity and energy was transforming the Australian jazz scene, and that these three musicians were contributing to it.

There are a number of remarkable aspects to the Australian contemporary jazz scene that should warrant at least modest, but on-going coverage in our print media. Yet, while review coverage is limited, non-review coverage of jazz seems destined to be restricted to occasional special jazz 'editions' of the what's-on supplements of newspapers, the kind of overview that appears every three or four years. A serious magazine like *The Monthly*, while covering opera and rock/pop, has ignored jazz from the very beginning, even though Melbourne, the magazine's home, can boast a jazz scene with the highest profile of any Australian city. Very occasionally, a 'jazz piece' might find its way into a fashion magazine: a bunch of fresh-faced young musicians modelling some modish gear, the backdrop to a fashion story. Sad to say, this might be the only way jazz can find exposure: our arts editors are either uninterested or struggling with increasingly tight budgets. Since most jazz writers are freelance, saving on their contributions remains a tempting option.

The lack of interest in jazz in the domestic media is shameful, because the growing impact of Australian modern and contemporary jazz is widely acknowledged overseas. How many arts editors/writers know that The Necks, whose CD *Townsville* was named one of 2007's Top Ten jazz releases by the influential British music magazine *The Wire*, are a cult band that regularly features on jazz festival programs and sells out medium-sized concert halls in London and Europe; that veteran alto-saxophonist Bernie McGann is considered by many European critics, and increasingly by leading American jazz critics like John Litweiler and John Corbett,[2] a very important, original voice on his instrument; that in the London *Observer* British jazz critic Stuart Nicholson named pianist Aron Ottignon one of the 'sounds of jazz for the new millennium';[3] that pianists Mike Nock and Joe Chindamo are well-known and highly respected jazz musicians in Japan, a huge market for jazz. There are features galore about comedians or cabaret artists who make it to the Edinburgh Festival Fringe, but rarely about an Australian jazz group doing a tour with dates in three, four or five different festivals.

Throughout the 1990s Clarion Fracture Zone, Mike Nock, Bernie McGann, Wanderlust, Dale Barlow, Paul Grabowsky, and The catholics all performed on the international jazz festival circuit, and in 2004 Ten Part Invention played at the Chicago Jazz Festival, one of the most prestigious in the United States. No longer is it a rarity for an Australian group to perform at a major European festival, Australian groups having been featured regularly in European and Canadian festival programs since the late 1980s. In 2006, singer Kristin Berardi won another competition at Montreux, the Shure International Singing Competition, while a few months later Jasmine Nelson and Karlie Bruce were placed second and third in the Brussels Young Singers Competition, and young pianist Jackson Harrison became the first Australian to have a release on the prestigious Swiss label, hatArt.

There are too many such instances to list here, but there are also too many for them to be dismissed as of no significance. Clearly, something important is happening on the scene from which these artists spring. So it is not unreasonable to ask why this activity is not being chronicled in the media. True, Kristin Berardi's success was the subject of an item on *The 7.30 Report*, but some say that that only happened because, behind the scenes, 'there was a friend who had a friend'. It wasn't a case of some open-minded ABC executive producer seeing the potential for a good arts story in a media release that came their way.

If the state of the Australian contemporary jazz scene in the mid-1980s were to be compared to what exists today, it would make startling reading. Over the last twenty years the Australian contemporary jazz scene has undergone a dramatic transformation and expansion, possibly unprecedented in the history of Australian arts. A major contemporary jazz scene has developed, almost *ex nihilo*, in Melbourne and is thriving, with internationally recognized musicians such as Paul Grabowsky, Scott Tinkler and Andrea Keller in prominent roles. By any number of measures—the number of musicians playing, the number of recordings being made, the extent of audience development, the level of touring both in Australia and overseas, the number of performance opportunities in cities where once there were none, the respect Australian musicians command overseas—contemporary jazz is flourishing.

And yet, at the same time, it is not. For all Melbourne's strength and vitality, most musicians are still only able to eke out the barest of living: four to six performances in Melbourne may still only generate a total of $350-$500. The scene in Sydney, which still boasts the country's largest concentration of contemporary jazz musicians, is in crisis: venues close and no new ones take their place. Despite all the changes that can be seen in Brisbane, there is still too little money and too few performance opportunities to talk of stable growth. The level of activity of the main contemporary jazz organizations may be impressive, but only by relying heavily on volunteers. Finally, despite the availability of assistance funding, national tours are rarely profitable, and in too many cases the musicians themselves end up out of pocket. Rock musicians are not the only ones who pay to play.

Lacking the financial clout that comes from having a mass audience like that enjoyed by pop/rock music, and without the cultural prestige of classical music that attracts relatively generous levels of funding and corporate sponsorship, jazz finds it hard to acquire the public profile it deserves. It exists on the margins of arts discourse and few Australians are aware of the achievements of so many of its principal artists.

In the new millennium the Australian jazz sector is a 'permanent underground'—financially unstable, with a frail jazz culture and weak infrastructure. All three elements—and they are interdependent—must be improved dramatically, if jazz is to be assured of a sustainable future, let alone achieve its potential as a vibrant, creative and original force in Australian music.

In this essay I want to describe the present state of the contemporary jazz scene,[4] examine the principal internal and external problems that afflict it and suggest the type of collective response the jazz community needs to make, in order to address them successfully.

2

Recent history

The late 1950s are usually considered the critical moment for modern jazz in Australia, when two very important venues, Jazz Centre 44 in Melbourne and the El Rocco Jazz Cellar in Sydney, opened within a short period of each other. A few years later, as part of a worldwide surge of interest in jazz, Australia experienced a strong revival of traditional jazz that also had echoes in Europe and the US. However, in general, the traditional revival in Continental Europe and in America was seen as a quaint aberration in the evolution of a music relentlessly driven forward by innovators such as Miles Davis, Ornette Coleman, Andrew Hill, John Coltrane, Cecil Taylor and Charlie Mingus.

Throughout the 1960s Sydney became a magnet for musicians, as the licensed social and sporting clubs offered many lucrative work opportunities. In some of the clubs the music played was jazz, in others it was commercial big-band arrangements to back variety artists. From the ranks of these commercial musicians came Sydney's comparatively large pool of modern jazz players.

But not all jazz musicians managed to secure commercial work. Some taught, while others had more menial day jobs. Avant-garde pianist Serge Ermoll's was more exciting than most: a 5th Dan black belt in karate, he did private detective work. On one occasion he was hired by the wife of a philandering fellow jazz musician who had run off to Melbourne with a showgirl. Ermoll tracked him down and brought him back to Sydney by car, handcuffing him to the wheel during meal breaks.

There were tours by overseas jazz artists, attempts to organize jazz festivals modelled on overseas events like the Newport Jazz Festival and recordings by the best-known jazz musicians. ABC Radio had several hours of jazz programming and employed a studio band that included many of Australia's finest jazz musicians. By then, Don Burrows was the best-known modern jazz musician in Australia, though Errol Buddle and Judy Bailey were also familiar to a wider public.

All this was only a pale reflection of the situation in Europe, of course, where modern jazz had a tremendous public profile. By the early part of the decade, Paris, London, Copenhagen and other European cities had already developed strong modern jazz scenes that attracted artists, intellectuals and students. Jazz music still had to fight for acceptance as an art form in the US, where the issue of recognition was inextricably entwined with that of race, but in Europe its position as a creation of modernism and as part of the avant-garde was not seriously disputed. The 1960s saw the European jazz festival scene take off, while at the end of the decade publicly-funded venues for jazz and improvised music, such as Amsterdam's BIMHUIS, started to appear. Already, there were well-established networks of agents, with promoters developing extensive touring circuits across the entire continent, while jazz was featured regularly in the mainstream media and in a string of serious, well-written and well-produced, specialist magazines.

Unfortunately, this type of integration of jazz infrastructure, culture and performance was entirely absent here. Australia, existing on the edge of Western arts activity, took longer to adopt and adapt worthwhile developments from abroad. No modern jazz festivals became established events, and there were few promoters or agents. The uneconomic nature of jazz touring in this period meant that few modern groups ever played outside their city of residence. Recordings by the key modern musicians/bands of the period were not numerous, but they were often recorded for major labels and so at least gained national distribution. However, in Australia's largest city, the only one with a significant modern jazz scene, 1969 saw the audience for that music lose its showcase venue—though, as its name implies, the room was dug out of rock—when the El Rocco closed.[5]

The 1970s

It took some time to fill the void left by the closure of El Rocco, but once The Basement opened in late 1973 there was a resurgence of modern jazz activity. Under the direction of Horst Liepolt, its booker and publicist, The Basement's program highlighted the most important local contemporary jazz groups on Monday and Tuesday nights, while the rest of the week was left to the Galapagos Duck, a jazz show-band who soon developed an enormous audience. John Clare's aptly-titled *Bodgie Dada and the Cult of Cool*—still the only narrative history of Australian modern jazz—vividly captures the sense of excitement and ferment in The Basement and the energetic optimism of Sydney's modern jazz scene throughout the 1970s.[6]

One of the most important developments early in the decade was the creation of a Jazz Studies course at the NSW Conservatorium of Music, through the efforts of Don Burrows and director Rex Hobcroft. Not only did this confer legitimacy on jazz, it also provided aspiring musicians with access to formal training and a qualification that would make them less reliant on commercial music work to earn a living.

The first Director of Jazz Studies was American saxophonist Howie Smith, whose arrival had an immediate impact on the local scene when he joined Roger Frampton and Phil Treloar in the Jazz Co-Op. This outstanding group developed a very strong following thanks to frequent appearances at The Basement, where Horst Liepolt brought an imaginative approach to promotion that had not been experienced in Sydney jazz before. Unusual ideas were given a chance and a special music night at The Basement occasionally resembled a cross between a 1920s Dadaist event and a 1960s Happening. The late singer Joe Lane's (in)famous *History of Jazz* concert started, with much moaning and intoning, at the dawn of creation, only reaching the swing era by the third set. Realising that time was short, he accelerated the tempo of proceedings, only to release whatever safety-valve had kept the audience under control. A near-riot ensued, in which people screamed, leapt from table-top to table-top and vaulted over chairs. Today, security guards would doubtless step in heavy-handedly. Then, however, we just went back to the bar for another drink.

Liepolt's activities had a profound effect in developing audiences for modern jazz both in Sydney and across Australia. He convinced a major record company to launch a jazz label under his direction ('44' Label) and he founded a new magazine, *Jazz Down Under*. (Importantly, both '44' and JDU had national distribution.) A born publicist, he was constantly on the lookout for opportunities to expose jazz in the commercial media and through the ABC. He organized concerts and mini jazz festivals in Sydney, convinced the nascent Sydney Festival to include a substantial component of local and overseas jazz groups in its programming and he helped establish the Manly Jazz Festival. Not all of Sydney's jazz community welcomed these changes, and in January 1977, at the Qantastic Jazz Festival held in the old Paddy's Markets, one band was pelted with fruit and eggs for being 'too way-out'.

After splitting with The Basement in 1978 Liepolt opened the Paradise Jazz Cellar in King's Cross, where, to attract a new audience, his programming focused on a younger generation of musicians (including the young James Morrison, who, while studying in the daytime at the Conservatorium, played there night after night till 4.00 a.m.). It was a logical move, but it reduced the opportunities for musicians such as Roger Frampton, Bernie McGann, Judy Bailey and others who, just a few years earlier, had been the stars of The Basement's program.

The 1970s also saw the foundation of several organizations that were to exert a considerable influence on jazz in Australia. In 1973, the Perth Jazz Society (PJS) was formed and, in Sydney in 1974, the Jazz Action Society (JAS), which spawned many sister organizations across the country, some of them still active today. In 1979, a group of emerging musicians, inspired by the avant-garde activities of the Association for the Advancement of Creative Musicians in Chicago, formed the Keys Music Association (KMA).

The KMA was the first modern jazz musicians' initiative in Australia and the forerunner of similar organizations active today. Both the KMA and JAS were early recipients of public funding to support their concert-based activities, establishing a pattern that other jazz-presenting organizations soon followed. Private promoters began utilising the Australia Council's Visiting Teacher Program to organize jazz summer-schools with American jazz clinicians and other musicians. The role of public funding in Australian jazz was soon to become crucial to its development, indeed its survival.

In terms of public profile, the decade of the 1970s marked a high point for modern jazz in Sydney: not only did three journalists in the Murdoch-owned press have their own jazz columns, but jazz was covered in the *National Times*, and also, in the mid-1970s, by the much-loved 'Ferret', the quality independent weekly *Nation Review*.

In 1981 Horst Liepolt left for New York, where he became a successful promoter and jazz-club owner. It should be remembered that Liepolt was first and foremost an entrepreneur who liked jazz, and his business, which he closed before emigrating, was a one-person operation. Sadly, though he had a profound effect on the development of Australian jazz during his time here, little of what he created survived his departure—neither the magazine, nor the record label, nor the jazz club (The Paradise closed in 1984), nor the concerts, while his successors at The Basement were never knowledgeable jazz fans, and they steadily wound down the jazz content of its program. It was for others to learn from his achievements and use what they learnt in the creation of new forms of support for jazz in the following decades.

The 1980s

Until 1983, the contemporary jazz scene was characterized by the same energy and creativity that had vitalised the second half of the 1970s. These were the years when the KMA reached the peak of its promotional activity and when the tours and educational efforts by (principally) US jazz artists made January in Sydney and Melbourne look like a month-long jazz festival. However, oversupply—too many promoters and too many groups appearing all at once—finally destroyed these 'jazz summers', as one promoter after another (including the Sydney Festival) lost money. After the 1983 event, the Sydney Festival brought no major jazz groups to Sydney and, as several venues opened and closed in rapid succession, the Sydney contemporary scene soon entered a period of crisis not unlike that following the closure of El Rocco.

However, there were other, more promising, developments. Pianist Judy Bailey thought that jazz needed a professional administrator to provide an information bank about the jazz scene, give advice to musicians and organizations, and lobby on behalf of jazz—and proposed the idea of a NSW Jazz Co-ordinator. In 1982, with funding from the Australia Council and the NSW Government, the position was established. (I myself was associated with the management committee of this association, either as a committee-member or as vice-president, from 1985 to 2002.) The program was replicated in other states, until, by 1985, there were jazz co-ordinators in every state, some of them also acting as jazz promoters. Eric Myers, already the NSW Co-ordinator, became the National Co-ordinator. This was Australia's first national service organization.

In the years that followed, new jazz-presenting organizations were quickly established. In 1983, Martin Jackson formed the Melbourne Jazz Co-operative (MJC) and the following year, I myself, with

Eric Myers' assistance, and with several other jazz enthusiasts, formed the Sydney Improvised Music Association (SIMA), a non-profit association, to foster and facilitate the performance of contemporary jazz music. Both organizations wanted to create greater performance opportunities for modern and contemporary jazz (bebop and beyond), styles they thought the private venues regarded as too risky to program, and which funded presenters such as the Jazz Action Societies neglected, preferring, at least in Sydney, to support mainstream jazz. Both SIMA and the MJC also intended to help emerging musicians develop an audience and to shift the focus of jazz coverage from the mainstream to the contemporary.

The creation of the MJC, SIMA, PJS and jazz co-ordination was a response to the failure of the private sector to take any risks in support of contemporary jazz. It was another important historical marker: from now on, non-profit presenting organizations utilising public funding would play an ever-increasing role in nurturing and sustaining contemporary jazz in Australia.

From the outset, the MJC's efforts were aided considerably by the *Age*'s jazz critic, Adrian (brother of Martin) Jackson. Armed with a deep knowledge of the music, familiar with the Australian jazz scene and developments overseas, sensitive to the domestic politics and aesthetic issues surrounding jazz, Jackson addressed his Melbourne readers clearly and authoritatively. In Sydney, contemporary jazz gained hugely from John Clare's appointment in 1987 as the *Sydney Morning Herald*'s jazz critic. Given sympathetic editors and not ungenerous space, Clare's witty and highly readable style reflected a profound commitment to, and understanding of, the music. But not everything was well: these positive developments were counteracted by the consistently hostile attitude to contemporary jazz of the *Australian*'s jazz writer, Kevin Jones.

The profile of jazz in the electronic media also gave cause for both celebration and concern. On its new FM network, the ABC had added several hours of programming with a much more contemporary flavour than was to be found on its long-established program on 2FC. On ABC-TV, however, the *Burrows Collection*, though the series ran for six years, included only two contemporary groups. But it did engage in a relentless promotion of James Morrison.[7] You might have thought the seventies had never been.

Throughout the 1980s, funding levels continued to increase not only for presenting organizations, but for ensembles such as Ten Part Invention, and, in the second half of the decade, applications for international touring and for recording also became more frequent. In the key centres of Sydney and Melbourne, applicants for funds came almost invariably from the contemporary sector.[8] By 1987, SIMA had expanded its program to two performances a week, but for a year or two the organization lacked a suitable permanent venue, until, in November 1989, it settled in the Strawberry Hills Hotel.

The increase in activity by the contemporary organizations was timely. In Sydney, the talent pool of musicians expanded rapidly, and in Melbourne, a new generation of contemporary jazz musicians, such as Paul Grabowsky, Jex Saarelaht and Ian Chaplin, was transforming the traditional jazz profile. In this context, two problems emerged that were to have long-term consequences. First, in committing to the support of performance, both SIMA and the MJC failed to invest properly in their own administration. Secondly, there was the problem of inadequate performance fees. Funding applications from jazz organizations, lodged by inexperienced administrators,[9] requested only very modest performance fees, and none at all for rehearsal. The argument that jazz musicians' fees should be commensurate with those paid to classical musicians was not mounted successfully. An unfortunate precedent was established and later, as funding became tighter, attempts to redress the situation predictably came to nothing.

The 1990s

Several important developments in the 1990s presented a challenge to the status of the jazz scene, to the security of its funding, to the resilience of its infrastructure and to the ability of its state-based organizations to work together when matters of common concern demanded concerted action. As the jazz co-ordination program established itself in New South Wales as a key element of infrastructure, its national offshoot was responsible for the production of a bi-monthly national newsletter, *Jazzchord*. Initially, *Jazzchord* was an information bulletin, but over time it broadened into a more wide-ranging publication and served to bring the jazz scene together. However, when that unity was tested, it failed. Moreover, in an hour of need, no leadership was shown by the senior co-ordination program either.

The test was over ABC Radio's decision, following a reorganization of programs in 1991, to cut jazz broadcast time by 35 per cent and to transfer all jazz programs to Classic-FM. This was a massive cut-back to a precious resource, yet it elicited no response from either the leading jazz organizations or the jazz co-ordinators—something which showed a lack of maturity as well as a reluctance to engage with large organizations on matters of importance to the well being of jazz. A few years later, when responsibility for funding the Australian Youth Orchestra had been transferred to the Commonwealth, the Music Board was faced with a cash shortfall. In the subsequent rounds many leading jazz organizations received significant cuts to their funding, with the comforting assurance that all longstanding applicants were sharing their pain. It was painful, indeed, to learn that many new music groups received significant increases. But once again no loud cries of protest were heard.

But, for all that, there was fresh cause for optimism and the growth across the sector in this period was marked, particularly in Sydney, where the *Sydney Morning Herald* enthused that Wanderlust, one of several exciting new ensembles of the day,[10] gave 'the distinct feeling that a full-blown movement had begun in Australian jazz'. Clearly, contemporary jazz still had a considerable fan-base. There was also a steady expansion of the contemporary scene in Melbourne, where the opening of Bennetts Lane Jazz Club in late

1992 was to have far-reaching consequences. Other positive indicators included the accelerating rate of recordings on new, dedicated jazz labels, increased touring opportunities, new jazz festivals, especially the Wangaratta Festival, the formation of new musician-run organizations in jazz and improvised music and new venues. Sydney, at this time, boasted five venues presenting a broad range of jazz styles from three to six nights a week.

Significant developments occurred in other major centres as well. In Brisbane, a group of musicians and enthusiasts formed the Music and Arts Club, which supported jazz and improvised music performance from 1988 to 1995. It helped transform the jazz music scene of a city of which traditional jazz had once been the mainstay. In Perth, an active presenting organization, an educational infrastructure based on the strong foundations of the West Australian Academy of Performing Arts (WAAPA)—with its commendable Bachelor of Music (Jazz) program—and a permanent youth jazz orchestra, drove an expansion of the modern jazz scene.

Other developments were less positive. It proved impossible to replicate Wangaratta's success with festivals in Melbourne, Sydney and on the Gold Coast. Moreover, the Sydney jazz scene was very soon to fall foul of a devastating trio of destructive forces, namely, restrictive licensing, high commercial rents and the ubiquitous poker machine.

In the second half of the 1990s differences of opinion arose over the direction the national co-ordination program should take. These led to needless internecine tensions between Sydney- and Melbourne-based organizations. The unfortunate outcome of this was that in late 1998, when, together with the Music Council of Australia, the NSW and National Jazz Co-ordination office produced a Strategic Plan for Jazz, its proposals were viewed with suspicion and its potential ignored. Richard Letts, Chair of the Music Council and the plan's principal author, commented: 'By the time everyone had defended their turfs from imagined take-overs or found some molehill to turn into a mountain, the outcome was paralysis.'[11]

In 2001 the Australia Council cut all funding to the NSW and national co-ordination programs. A year later the Victorian and SA programs were also cut. Despite assurances by Music Board officers that the decision was based 'on the points', suspicion remains that the Board, desperate to find money for new clients, saw in the jazz community's disunity an opportunity which it could not ignore. The Music Board must have known that only a year earlier the jazz co-ordination program had received high praise at a forum organized by the Australia Council. Marc Vasey, artistic director of the JAZZCITY Festival in Edmonton, Canada noted enviously,

> We do not have, however, a situation like you have here, where you have state officers who are charged with the challenge of trying to create a better and more organized jazz perspective in regional states. […] We don't even have a national jazz co-ordinator in Canada.[12]

The dismemberment of the NSW/National jazz co-ordination programs demonstrated that the jazz community was incapable of defending valuable, funded infrastructure and that it was perceived as weak and disunited. Though successful jazz co-ordination programs are still funded in West Australia, Queensland and South Australia, neither the national, nor the NSW or Victorian programs have been resurrected. Nor is there any advocacy for jazz at either a national level or in the major jazz states of Victoria and NSW. In view of the real paucity of performance opportunities there, the resurrection of such a program would be of considerable benefit to Sydney.

3

The end of jazz?

That Australia produces many fine young musicians is not in doubt. But does jazz itself have a future? Is it caught in a time warp, reproducing sets of musical gestures that are merely variations of past styles, of interest only to historians, sound archivists and devotees of nostalgia? Some who believe that jazz is a dead, or else a heritage, form say that 'improvisation' has supplanted it. For them, jazz is no longer the site of innovation, but a formalised tradition, that has forsaken experimentation in favour of 'eternal verities' such as the blues and swing rhythmic patterns. Non-jazz-based improvisation, on the other hand, offers many of the possibilities that staunch supporters of the jazz tradition have rejected: use of electronics and computers, use of multi-media in performance and so on.

The argument that jazz is dead has its roots in the 1960s and 1970s, in the debates among British and European avant-garde jazz musicians, seeking to theorize a space for their work where it wouldn't be subject to endless comparisons with the practices of American jazz musicians.[13] The process of rejection followed in stages: first, American jazz was rejected as a model, then rhythm and melody, then the idea of jazz itself. The rhetoric of the debate was po-litically right-minded, born of a wish to create new musical forms that were explicitly anti-capitalist, anti-imperialist and anti-racist. Even at the time, some prominent musicians thought the exclusion of all jazz elements from a new improvised music was nothing short of a new orthodoxy. And today, echoes of the argument that jazz has run its course can still be heard in Australia.[14]

Jazz musician, improviser and critic Roger Dean takes a more generous and considered approach to the relationship between jazz and non-jazz-based improvised music.[15] While espousing the cause of today's avant-garde, he doesn't dismiss improvis-ers—saxophonist Sandy Evans, for instance—who still work within the jazz tradition and consider it open, flexible and dynamic.

For certain American musicians, like cornetist/ trumpeter Graham Haynes, jazz as represented by the tradition from Louis Armstrong to John Coltrane *is* dead and call for a re-engagement with popular forms such as hip-hop and electronic dance music.[16] Rather than champion 'improvisation', they believe that the future of jazz lies in working with popular forms, or rather, with forms popular in America.

In English critic Stuart Nicholson's view, the American jazz scene is caught in permanent stasis, partly because the highly influential musician Wynton Marsalis has steered the music into an aesthetic cul-de-sac, and partly because its high-fee, private jazz-education system with its high staff/student ratios permits little time for the nurturing of individuality.[17] For Nicholson, the really vibrant, innovative jazz is being played in Europe, where it has been taken seriously as an art form for decades and where adequate public funding enables artists and private entrepreneurs to take risks.

Much of what Nicholson writes about the creativity of the European and, especially, Scandinavian jazz scenes could apply equally to Australia—except, of course, their very high levels of funding. Here, the American style wars caused only a ripple because the deeper aspects of the issues involved—such as race—had no social foundation. Today, Australian contemporary jazz musicians are open to engaging with any music which interests them, from noise/rock (Bucketrider) to Afro-Cuban (Barney McAll), music from New Guinea (Aaron Choulai), music of the Pacific Islands (Aron Ottignon), minimalist influenced improvisation (The Necks and Band of Five names) to name but a few. Their creativity deserves more than admiration; it deserves support.

Roger Dean asserts that Australian contemporary jazz has not only found its own voices, but that

> [it] has again become highly influential in the development of Australian music, no matter how 'inaudible' it has remained, [...] its contributions go far beyond what would be expected of a small country in quality and range. From a period of largely imitative modern jazz, we have emerged with a vibrant heterodoxy which can compete with that of any country or region. Its only problems are those of exposure, travel, distance and 'free trade'.[18]

Dean is not the only observer to have reached this conclusion. Richard Letts has also commented in a similar vein on the quality of jazz music produced in Australia.[19]

4

It's all different

What would a series of snapshots of the current Australian contemporary jazz scene reveal? I have suggested over the last several decades an irregular pattern of growth and development has been counterbalanced by considerable reverses and difficulties. At present, only Melbourne's jazz scene (and perhaps Brisbane's) seems to have consolidated all the gains made in the last decade, learnt from the failures and is enjoying a period of stability and development. To elicit perceptions of their local scene as well as suggestions as to how things might be improved, in 2007 I invited a number of key people involved in the QLD, WA and SA jazz scenes to complete a questionnaire.[20]

The results indicated that of all the cities Melbourne provides the most performance venues, and that in Bennetts Lane it boasts Australia's leading jazz club. Furthermore, and in addition to this, the high profile of jazz in Melbourne is due to the publicity generated by large- and small-scale events such as the Melbourne International Jazz Festival (MIJF), the Stonnington Jazz and the Melbourne International Women's Jazz Festival. Additionally, the regional Wangaratta Festival of Jazz and Blues, widely considered Australia's leading jazz festival, receives extensive local and national media coverage. The Wangaratta Festival sponsors the instrumental competition known as the National Jazz Awards, while MIJF's associated event is the Australian Jazz Awards.

Sydney, by contrast, is facing a severe crisis in performance opportunities, occasioned by the forces mentioned earlier: a restrictive licensing system (liberalised under new legislation[21]), high commercial rents and pub poker machines. As a result, in the last three years, no new jazz venues have been opened by the private sector to replace those that have closed. This has left the country's largest concentration of jazz musicians with an ever-declining number of opportunities to perform and develop their audience.

They are obliged to rely increasingly on the showcase performances provided by SIMA and the JazzGroove Association. But the modest funding of these organizations prevents them from stepping into the breach left by the closure of venues.

There are several jazz festivals in Sydney, of course, but these are smaller, with tiny budgets compared to those of Melbourne/Victoria. The long-running Manly Jazz Festival has always suffered from a lack of suitable indoor venues and a narrow financial base, while Jazz: Now, jointly produced by SIMA, JazzGroove and the Studio, Sydney Opera House, is a boutique event with limited potential to expand. In 2001, thanks to the philanthropy of Lawrence and Kathy Freedman, the Freedman Jazz Fellowship was added to Sydney's jazz calendar. Worth $15,000, it is the richest competitive jazz prize in Australia. It is ironic that, as opportunities to perform in Sydney have diminished, it is Sydney-based musicians that have always dominated both this award and, since 1990, the National Jazz Awards at Wangaratta.

Brisbane's contemporary jazz scene has grown rapidly, but from a very much smaller base. The city now boasts two excellent jazz festivals along with a service/presenting organization that works hard on limited funding to meet the needs of the jazz scene. While the pool of musicians remains small, the educational institutions that teach jazz turn out high-quality students: Kristin Berardi, for example, who last year added the Freedman Fellowship to her victory at Montreux in 2006, is from Queensland. There is also a core of jazz-improvising musicians of exceptional ability—saxophonist Elliott Dalgleish, violinist John Rodgers and drummer Ken Eadie, to name but a few—who may tour internationally, but choose to base themselves in Queensland, rather than in one of the major jazz centres. In the main, Brisbane has no lack of quality players, only of financial resources and suitable venues.

By comparison, the Perth scene is relatively well-funded, has stable, well-established service/presenting organizations and in the West Australian Youth Jazz Orchestra, founded in 1982, boasts Australia's only orchestra with a permanent training program. In 1999, the legendary Frank Foster, former leader of the Count Basie Orchestra, became a patron. However, Perth has no jazz festival and—again, insufficient venues—depressing circumstances for both graduating WAAPA students and mid-career musicians.

It's the same story in Adelaide, where, in spite of the fact that it was there that *JazzScene* began publication in 1995, the jazz scene itself has been particularly slow to develop since then. However, it has a presenting/service organization (JazzSA) that has recently undergone renewal, and together with the musicians' initiative Creative Original Music Adelaide (COMA), established in 2006—and Paul Grabowsky's assumption of the artistic directorship of the Adelaide Festival from 2010—there may be signs that things in the south are looking up.

At present, there are no advocacy or service organizations operating at the national level. Nor have Sydney and Melbourne had a service organization since the demise of their respective jazz co-ordination programs early in the millennium. The urgency of the need for a new, national advocacy body cannot be overstated, for the simple reason that none of the existing jazz organizations can afford to allocate their scarce resources to advocacy.

A fundamental problem is the size of the jazz-sector organizations. Apart from the festivals, they are small or medium-sized enterprises, and suffer from the problems afflicting all small-to-medium arts organizations. In 2002, the *Report to Ministers on an Examination of the Small-to-Medium Performing Arts Sector* described the work of the sector as a 'pivotal contribution [. . .] to cultural vitality and diversity'. However, it pointed out that the characteristics of the small-to-medium sector companies included a commitment to emphasise artistic development at the cost of audience development; to rely on volunteers (both a strength and a weakness); to generate low surpluses; to have a limited administrative capacity; to attract very limited sponsorship and to have only a narrow scope for attracting more.[22]

Furthermore, the *Report* demonstrated that over the period of the study, 1998–2000, the financial health of organizations working in Dance and Music had deteriorated, and that the entire small-to-medium Music sub-sector ran at an increasing loss. Triennially-funded organizations revealed a higher level of surplus than those funded on different models, but the *Report* provided no further information in relation to the Music sub-sector—except to draw the self-evident conclusion that it is under-resourced! Since up till the time of writing (February 2008) only three jazz organizations had ever been funded triennially, the success of other funded companies at running positive bottom lines must have been modest. Moreover, the extra funding that jazz companies received in the Howard Government's additional allocation in the 2007 budget did little to improve their overall financial position.

5

Jazz in the media: fear or loathing?

I n Europe, where jazz continues to enjoy a high status, the media devote considerable space and time to its coverage. In August 2006, the French radio station *France* broadcast a multi-part series on jazz and the prestigious daily, *Le Monde*, carried an illustrated review, two-thirds of a page long, of the Keith Jarratt Trio.[23] Just below this, with a much smaller photograph, was an enthusiastic review of a Rolling Stones concert. I have no wish to argue the merits of these two groups, simply to observe that, unlike Australia's, where a recent survey has suggested that classical music and operate predominate,[24] the French newspaper coverage of music seems not to be dominated by pop and rock music.

In Australia, jazz is not accorded the same respect as the other arts. Non-specialist writers are often assigned to cover jazz, the coverage is inconsistent, jazz reviews are rarely accompanied by photographs, and there are very few feature articles on specific aspects of the scene. John McBeath, who writes for the *Australian* and the *Adelaide Advertiser*, is competent, with a good knowledge of the music. However, as he is based in Adelaide, whose jazz scene is the smallest and the least dynamic of all the mainland capitals', he is poorly placed to hear the leading groups/musicians or to experience at first hand new currents of activity. Sydney-based Mathew Westwood also covers jazz for the *Australian*. However, he is a classical music specialist with little knowledge of jazz and therefore his work, no matter how professional, is not grounded in a deep knowledge of the subject. Would the *Australian*'s arts editor appoint non-specialists to cover classical music, theatre or dance? That the editor of the *West Australian* was happy to have a non-specialist review the great jazz pianist Herbie Hancock's concert in Perth last April is little short of insulting.

The popular papers of the Murdoch stable such as the *Telegraph* and *Sunday Telegraph* in Sydney and the *Courier-Mail* in Brisbane do not cover jazz—indeed, their arts coverage in general is minimal. The *Herald Sun* and *Sunday Herald Sun* carry CD reviews and cover the major jazz festivals in Victoria, but have no on-going coverage of the live scene.

In John Clare and John Shand the *Sydney Morning Herald* has the country's two leading jazz critics. While Shand is the principal reviewer of live performances and a feature writer, both review CDs. Until late in 2007, when the frequency of all reviews declined, the *SMH* ran about three jazz reviews per month. However, jazz features had all but disappeared from the arts pages a decade earlier, and from mid-2000 they disappeared from 'The Metro' entertainment supplement as well. The *Age* continues with jazz reviews and features in its arts section, but 'EG', its entertainment guide, is almost devoid of jazz coverage.

Beyond the newspapers, most jazz writing is limited to CD reviews in hi-fi magazines, or to 'a round-up of the scene' columns, such as in the magazine *Rhythms*. Since the mid-1990s, jazz CD reviews have been dropped from the Australian edition of *Rolling Stone*, the *Bulletin* and the *Australian Financial Review*, all national, high-profile publications, where taste omnivores might have sought them out.

There is no need to discuss jazz coverage on commercial radio or television: there isn't any. Indeed, there's little arts coverage of any sort. The public sphere, however, is different. ABC and community radio provide a markedly brighter picture, with community radio in particular broadcasting hundreds of hours of jazz programming nationally each week. Stations 3PBS and 2RES, for example, have impressive jazz schedules, with keen, knowledgeable presenters, although it is not hard to find 'jazz' programs that are nothing more than vehicles for musical nostalgia. A real concern could be the absence or extremely low level of jazz programming by youth-oriented stations such as FBI and 2SER in Sydney, 3RRR and syn90.7 in Melbourne or edgeradio 90.7 in Hobart.

ABC Radio makes a vital contribution to Australian jazz through its broadcasting, and its recording of local jazz: in 2006-07 the organization made 65 studio and live jazz recordings, most featuring home-grown artists.[25] Gerry Koster's 'Jazz Up Late', created in 2006 to complement Mal Stanley's 'Jazztrack', lifted Classic-FM's weekly jazz quota to six hours, an allocation close to what it had been in 1991, before cut-backs were implemented, while another welcome addition is the web-based station, digJazz. On his Radio National 'Music Show', Andrew Ford includes interviews with overseas jazz musicians and critics and on occasion includes CD reviews by the *Age*'s jazz and world music writer Jessica Nicholas. 'The Planet' has considerable jazz content and 'Into the Music' occasionally focuses on jazz, while Tim Ritchie's 'Sound Quality' includes electronic and hybrid forms such as nu jazz. Triple-J continues to overlook jazz, except on 'Sound Lab', where crossover jazz/electronica tracks can occasionally be heard. Sadly, Radio National's arts programs have generally ignored the jazz scene and that is true of most ABC local radio.

While 'Jazz Up Late' is a welcome addition, further expansion is surely justified and perhaps some guidelines in relation to jazz on all ABC radio stations ought to be considered. Any new jazz programs should modify the 'disc-spinning' format currently prevailing on 'Jazz Track' and 'Jazz Up Late', in favour of one that brings audience, artists and the entire jazz scene closer together through interviews and discussion.

The current situation with regard to jazz on television offers little consolation. In recent years SBS has downplayed its commitment to cultural diversity. Indeed, somewhat ironically perhaps, from its early days, the multi-cultural broadcaster has privileged European high culture over jazz, a music that is a cultural hybrid. The programs that have found their way onto its schedule have been largely 'historical-biographical', documentaries featuring great musicians of the past, such as that broadcast in June 2005 of Miles Davis's great 1970 Isle of Wight concert. The jazz of today is ignored, despite the abundance of recent concert footage available.

In recent years ABC-TV's record has been very poor indeed. In 2000 it screened one jazz series on Australian jazz, 'The Pulse', and in 2002 'Jazz', Ken Burn's controversial 10-part, social history of 'America's music'. ABC-TV has seemed incapable of creating any quality, non-pop/rock music programs other than telecasts of operas and symphony concerts. This may reflect a lack of will in budgetary allocation, but it is unlikely to be a question of resources, as the ABC allocates considerable funds for J-TV to film concerts by rock/pop bands in regional areas. The content of live broadcasts and the live music content of arts programs such as 'Sunday Arts' show a fearful lack of imagination, vision and curiosity. Material that isn't pop/rock or classical or perhaps 'quirky' is excluded. The new 2007 television series, 'SET' is described on the ABC web site as 'a bold new live perform-ance-based music program featuring the very best of Australia's vibrant and experimental music scene [...] sometimes neglected by the mainstream media'.[26] The idea was good and the 25-minute duration of each episode allowed enough time for each artist/band to say something meaningful. However, certain of presenter Kate Crawford's programming choices, such as Francis Plagne, for instance, were puzzling, while others, like The Necks, could not possibly be considered experimental, or under-exposed. 'SET' is a step forward and it very much deserves to survive, though with some development. The creation of 'SET' hardly undermines the case for a separate jazz program. In fact, it strengthens the case for the ABC to produce a number of new programs devoted to music in order to overcome its dire record in this area.

Let's imagine the contribution that could be made to jazz and new music by a different program, one in which jazz, new music and some pop/rock come together: in one episode Elision and Ten Part Invention might perform two pieces each; in another, solo performers such as percussionist Claire Edwardes, trumpeter Scott Tinkler, pianists Michael Kieran Harvey and Chris Abrahams of The Necks all perform; and a third might feature the James Muller Trio and the John Butler Trio. Let them perform before an invited studio audience, and engage Tim Freedman, a rock musician with eclectic tastes, to host the series. It could attract a new audience.

In recent years, the pay-TV arts station Ovation has broadcast live concert footage from jazz festivals, live studio performances and jazz documentaries. All of this material is sourced overseas: no local product has been shown. Nevertheless, the channel has an impressive track record in the area of jazz broadcasting that easily surpasses that of both the ABC and

SBS. So it was both saddening and surprising that, soon after a management buy-out, jazz content virtually disappeared from Ovation's 2007 program schedules. Repeated attempts on my part, both by email and telephone, to discover the reason for such a dramatic downgrading of jazz have failed to elicit any response.

The virtual absence of jazz from public and pay television contributes significantly to its low profile. Jazz performance is poorly suited to the music clip format and so there is little likelihood of a jazz equivalent of 'rage' reaching our screens. The only alternative for television is the purchase of filmed concert or club performances from overseas. These are readily available, but the ABC, SBS and now, it seems, Ovation[27] as well, seem no more interested in purchasing them than in investing money in filming the domestic product. Their current negative attitude has closed another avenue by which the public might have encountered jazz, and local musicians enhanced their audience.

Others could be cited, but these examples should be sufficient illustration of the uneven nature of jazz coverage in the Australian media. Back in 1987, jazz historian Bruce Johnson observed: 'The relative position of jazz in Australian culture continues to be anomalous.'[28] Sadly, he could have written these words two decades later.

6

Funding jazz:
Please, sir ...

t is beyond the scope of this essay to undertake
either a detailed analysis of the funding allocated to
jazz by various sources or an extended commentary
on issues of comparative equity with respect to other,
funded music sectors. What is possible, however, is
a consideration of jazz funding in New South Wales,
the state which, in SIMA and Jazzgroove, has jazz-
presenting organizations in receipt of the highest
combined level of funding across the sector from all
sources ($150,000 in 2007). I shall then examine
current Australia Council funding, and seek to draw
some appropriate comparisons and conclusions.

I have included in the NSW figures those grants
awarded to improvised music, since this related idiom
frequently involves musicians who perform / play
jazz. While including grants to improvised music
inflates the total allocation, it also underscores its
modest nature. I have not included grants to major
companies such as the Sydney Symphony Orchestra,
the Brandenburg Orchestra or the Australian Chamber
Orchestra.

Table 1 compares jazz funding to new music funding, another minority music form. The totals for new
music include allocations to ensembles, to service

organizations, and to organizations on behalf of ensembles and individual artists. However, grants to dance and theatre companies for music commissions and/or recordings, or for the creation of multi-media works employing musicians, are not included.

Table 1: Arts NSW funding to jazz/improvised music and new music[29]

	2003	2004	2005	2006	2007
SIMA	47,800	53,000	55,000	55,000	65,000
JazzGroove	17,000	17,000	20,000	25,000	30,000
Jazz & Improv (total)	106,800	88,000	97,000	104,000	136,000
New Music	292,000	324,000	387,600	380,000	374,000

These figures reveal a generally upward trend: the relatively higher total of $106,800 for jazz in 2003 is accounted for by a one-off project grant of $25,0000, but the base figure remains low. Until 2002, Arts NSW, the NSW Government's arts policy and funding body, also supported the NSW Jazz Co-ordination Program, its final grant one of $25,000. Currently, the principal jazz clients are SIMA and the JazzGroove Association, but support is also given to the Bellingen Jazz Festival and several other, smaller applicants.

For 2007, the total funding for Music from ArtsNSW, excluding allocations to major companies, was $1,650,000. The total funding for jazz and improvised music was $136,000, of which SIMA received $65,000, JazzGroove $30,000 and Machine for Making Sense $20,000,[30] while new music grants totalled $374,000. Jazz/improvisation represents 8 per cent of the total, while new music, accounting for 23 per cent of the total, attracted 2.72 times as much funding as jazz. In fact, the combined funding for jazz and improvised music is less than that of The Song Company, Sydney's prestigious vocal ensemble.[31]

What about the Australia Council's support for jazz? According to Kate Lidbetter, the AC's Director, Music, grants to the jazz sector represent 15 per cent of the Music Board's total funding, about the same as the allocation to new and popular music.[32] Grants to the major service/presenting organizations for 2008 come to $396,000. The principal beneficiary, the Australian Art Orchestra (AAO), received $118,000. While the AAO is not strictly a jazz ensemble, I include it here because it both employs jazz musicians and includes jazz in its repertoire.[33]

In spite of the dip in 2002, as Table 2 shows, the general level of funding has increased steadily over the last seven years. Yet the level remains low. The main presenting organizations in Sydney and Melbourne account for about 350 performances each year, yet, if the grants to SIMA, the MJC and JazzGroove from the Australia Council are added to the grants allocated them by ArtsNSW and Arts Victoria, the total is less than $300,000.[35] This is a very modest amount.

I noted earlier that Australia Council funding to jazz accounted for 15 per cent of the Music Board's total allocation, the same percentage as for new and pop/rock music. Analysing the allocations for 1995–96, Bruce Johnson found that jazz accounted for 15 per cent of the Australia Council's total disbursement to music.[36] Certainly, since then, while the

Table 2: Australia Council core funding to principal jazz organizations[34]

	2001	2002	2003	2004	2005	2006	2007	2008
Jazz Western Australia	20,000	20,000	25,000	28,000	35,000	47,000	47,000	55,000
Jazz South Australia	20,000	20,000	10,000	15,000	nil	nil	15,000	25,000
Melbourne Jazz Co-op	26,000	26,000	30,000	32,500	37,000	40,000	40,000	50,000
National / NSW Jazz Co-ordination	50,000	nil	nil	nil	nil	nil	nil	nil
SIMA	34,000	38,000	32,000	35,000	40,000	45,000	40,000	60,000
Jazzgroove	nil	10,000	10,000	10,000	12,500	15,000	15,000	25,000
Jazz Queensland	15,000	20,000	17,850	15,000	20,000	20,000	20,000	23,000
Wangaratta Festival of Jazz and Blues	25,000	25,000	25,000	25,000	25,000	30,000	35,000	40,000
Australian Arts Orchestra	85,000	95,000	95,000	95,000	112,000	112,000	112,000	118,000
Total	275,000	228,000	254,850	255,000	286,500	309,000	324,000	396,000

monies allocated to jazz by the Music Board and its predecessors have increased, for some organizations this has not always been the case. However, that figure of 15 per cent figure is troubling. Are the jazz and new music sectors the same size? How is it that pop/rock music, a commercial form that has made successful applications for about five years now, has, in such a short time, attained the same level of funding as jazz? Are there invisible ceilings that determine the amount of funding going to various sectors? These are questions that demand answers, and it is simply not good enough to issue the standard 'Decisions were based on the quality of the applications', a statement designed to forbid any challenge. Moreover, looking at the current picture, is jazz a larger, smaller, or similar-sized music form in comparison to new music? Is it by mere coincidence that it attracts the same percentage of Music Board funds?

The exact amount of public money allocated to the jazz sector differs slightly from year to year, but reasonable estimates can be made.[37] The single largest grant is that made to the Melbourne International Jazz Festival by the Victorian Major Events Corporation. The precise amount has never been disclosed, but is widely believed to be between $200,000 and $300,000 per year. Let us err on the side of generosity and say that it is $300,000. If all the published grants are totalled, and a guesstimate made where precise information is lacking, it seems fair to suggest that the total allocation of public money made to the jazz sector amounts to no more than $1.3m per year. This is not a lot. It is small wonder that Bruce Johnson and Roger Dean have asserted that jazz in Australia is underfunded.[38]

The consequences of these low funding levels are far-reaching and are reflected in vital areas: the low fees paid to artists by jazz-presenting organizations (and many festivals); the low level of marketing and promotional spend; the relatively low administrative salaries payable in the sector; the need to rely on voluntary work; the inability of jazz organizations to afford rents, and, as a consequence, the inconvenient location of their offices.

Let me consider each of these in turn. SIMA, which pays the highest fees of any presenting organization in the country, can only manage a standard fee of $170 per musician per performance, with a small leader's premium of $10. The minimum fee paid to a musician travelling from interstate for a SIMA-sponsored performance varies from $180 to $250. All rehearsals are unpaid.

Since 1999, SIMA has staged performances on Friday and Saturday nights. These are generally agreed to be the optimum nights for attracting audiences, but also those when most commercial opportunities for musicians occur, either corporate 'gigs' or other forms of commercial music (some even commercial jazz) such as rock cover bands, show bands or bands backing variety performers. In Sydney, although the fees for such commercial work start at $200, musicians will tell you that they usually receive $250 and above. In order to play jazz, a musician who accepts a SIMA engagement may need to make a financial loss. Indeed, very good musicians—even a bass player with the international experience of Jonathan Zwartz—have been obliged to withdraw from jazz performances because they simply could not afford to make the financial sacrifice.

The inadequacy of artists' fees, whether paid by funded jazz organizations or private entrepreneurs (such as jazz venues), is something remarked upon by all the respondents to the questionnaire referred to earlier. The average fee cited was $150, sometimes less, a figure corresponding to those published by Bruce Johnson and Shane Homan in 2002. In a survey conducted by Johnson and Homan and covering the previous half-decade, Sydney musicians—including some of our most distinguished and high-profile jazz musicians—responded that well over half their income came from non-jazz work.[39]

Unpaid rehearsals present a further problem. There is considerable anecdotal evidence of musicians missing unpaid rehearsals in favour of a paid engagement elsewhere. In other cases, a musician's evening performance might be affected by having been obliged to spend the entire day teaching or undertaking several commercial, i.e. income-generating, music engagements. One person's below-par performance is likely to affect the playing of the entire group. I speak from long experience when I say that such instances are not rare—and may well be getting more frequent.

The dearth of suitable venues continues to be a stumbling block in all the major jazz centres except Melbourne—though there are plenty of complaints there of poor rates of pay for musicians. One evening, the original Dizzy's Jazz Club (in the little post office in Richmond's Swan St) hired a band, failed to open its doors, and offered the musicians $100 each in compensation. One poster wrote on Ozjazzforum, 'I think […] Dizzy's model has a lot of merit. 100 bucks for not playing a note seems quite good, especially if you can put together three or four of those gigs in the same week.' Adelaide, Brisbane and Perth respondents to my questionnaire last year identified the lack of suitable venues or 'jazz hubs' as a serious problem, and I have noted that at the time there is not one full-time jazz club operating in Sydney. Since the creation of jazz venues has long been assumed to be the exclusive role of the private sector, the withdrawal of that sector from a key market such as Sydney must be considered a crisis. The changes made late in 2007 to the New South Wales liquor and entertainment licensing laws, intended to transform Sydney nightlife, are welcome and may tempt the private sector to invest in new jazz venues. However, it is difficult to predict how soon these changes to the law will have the desired effect. It is impossible to imagine the future of drama and dance performance being left to the whims and vagaries of the private sector.

Evidence of the low marketing spend of the jazz sector is easily found in the entertainment advertising pages of our newspapers. While special events such as festivals or tours by major overseas artists at venues like the Sydney Opera House, the Victorian Arts Centre or Adelaide's Festival Centre generate plenty of column-inches—full pages, even—of advertising, there are precious few mentions of jazz events from one week to the next in either the *Age* supplement (EG) or that of the *Sydney Morning Herald* (The Metro). Such a low level of advertising implies that the jazz sector not only has low visibility, but is also financially weak.

That weakness is further underlined by the poor salaries paid to administrators of jazz organizations. Most of these positions are part-time, and in one or two cases salaries are higher than those paid to part-time administrators in small music, dance and drama companies. Recently, for example, the New Music Network advertised a two-day-per-week administrative position for a mere $15,000 per annum. Several jazz organizations pay more for a two-day-a-week position, whereas others can only afford the same, or less. However, it must be remembered that the salaries paid by SIMA or the MJC or Jazz QLD or Jazz WA for part-time positions—with the rare exceptions of those paid to administrators of the larger jazz festivals—are the highest in the jazz sector. Poor salaries and the lack of full-time positions are the inevitable result of low funding levels, and constitute a serious disincentive for many otherwise energetic and ambitious would-be arts administrators. Even if a suitable candidate were to accept such a job, with its implicit demands for voluntary work and its increasingly time-consuming reporting requirements, it is hard to imagine them persevering in a position that offered inadequate remuneration and almost no career path. There are few like Eric Myers, who in 2001 and after nearly twenty years as the NSW and National jazz co-ordinator, was still working sixty-hour weeks, for a salary of $45,000.

A further disincentive for administrators is their work environment. The administrator of MJC works in a converted garage adjacent to his home; Jazzgroove has no office at all, while the office of SIMA is a windowless, converted storage room. Given the other, more urgent calls on their funds, these organizations are unwilling or, perhaps more likely, unable to afford more than a minimal rent.

These examples can all be directly attributed to low levels of funding. Furthermore, it is hard to believe that these conditions do not influence the way jazz organizations are generally perceived, even by supportive funding bodies.

7

Australian jazz culture

Every art form needs a burgeoning culture, which benefits from the activities developed by its enthusiasts—and this is true of jazz. These activities raise its public profile, and create opportunities for discussion, and fuel debate and advocacy. It is these events, arranged by arts organizations, which provide the vital link between artists and their audiences.

Australian jazz culture tries hard to fulfil these essential functions, but fails to do them well because it is weak, lacking in financial means and fragmented.

There is no quality national jazz publication. The last attempt at a jazz magazine, *Australian Jazz and Blues Magazine*, foundered in 1994 after eight issues. *JazzChord* ceased publication in 2002, after nine years, and the future of the national jazz web site, <Jazz. org.au>, which was funded by the Australia Council from 2004 to 2007, is currently uncertain. There are various newsletters and jazz sites, such as *Jazz Scene* and *Jazz and Beyond*, that try to give jazz a presence in print and on the web, but both have limited impact and need to attract funds to improve content and design. Other publications, such as *Quarterly Rag*, the various Jazz Action Societies' and regional jazz society newsletters, address special-interest groups within the jazz scene, but have limited distribution and few editorial resources.

The lack of a national magazine, or a web site with an editorial budget sufficient to buy high-quality content (reviews, features, discussion pieces), restricts even further the opportunities for paid work open to jazz writers and critics. At the level of academic research the problem is similar, and despite the important work of Bruce Johnson, especially his *Oxford Companion to Australian Jazz* (1987) and *The Inaudible Music* (2000), and of Roger Dean, in particular his *Sounds from the Corner: Australian Contemporary Jazz on CD since 1973* (2005), there still are relatively few books and articles published by Australian writers and researchers about the local and international jazz scene. And jazz-studies courses train students for careers in music performance and offer no positions for jazz scholars. The weakness of Australian jazz culture is yet another result of under-funding. Jazz organizations may be anxious to put something other than news of forthcoming events ('gigs of the week'), interviews with musicians and lists of favourite CDs on their web sites, but are financially constrained from doing so. Nor are they able to adequately promote themselves to generate the traffic to attract advertisers. Indeed, the level of discretionary funding in marketing and promotional budgets is too low to allow such organizations to advertise in any jazz publications that may approach them.

All this indicates a weak jazz culture that is incapable of raising the profile of jazz on the Australian performing arts landscape. It is not surprising that a successful group such as The Necks and a highly visible musician like Paul Grabowsky, both of whom emerged from the jazz milieu and continue to perform at jazz festivals, have both been careful to construct their public profiles by distancing themselves from the jazz scene. Their reasons for doing so may differ, but the implicit message about jazz that such a strategy sends out is clear enough: put crudely, an association with jazz is not a good look! Jazz culture and the jazz organizations have failed to establish jazz as an important element in the national arts discourse in Australia—with the result that its problems tend to get lost in those issues facing 'contemporary music in general'. Despite increased levels of funding from both commonwealth and state agencies, close examination reveals the fragile nature of the jazz sector and the dangers threatening its sustainability.

But this is not to say that our jazz sector is entirely without strengths. The quality of tertiary jazz education in Australia is high and has produced many very fine musicians. In other words, the *supply* column of our ledger (individual players, groups, students and graduates etc) is in order. We need now to look to the future needs of the sector and turn to the *demand* column (the audience, the organizations and infrastructure that deliver opportunities for musicians). It is these that are in need of support.

8

A modest plan

In reflecting on these issues, I have concluded that the jazz sector needs a National Jazz Plan (NJP), to guide the actions of the funding bodies and bring some strategic thinking into the work of our organizations. In 2001, a National Strategic Plan for Jazz Development (NSPJD), first drafted in 1998, was released by the National Jazz Co-ordination Office, with the support of the Music Council of Australia. Unfortunately, the National and NSW Jazz Co-ordination programs collapsed soon after; the old plan became the site of a power struggle and went into limbo.

The jazz community must not allow personal agendas or slow consultative processes to destroy another opportunity to take control of its future. A representative group must agree on the basic objectives, work quickly to develop appropriate strategies for implementation and then commence lobbying the relevant government bodies. David Throsby, who has described the process of creating policy documents as either top-down or bottom-up, comments that in creating cultural policy a top-down process 'smacks of a cultural elite telling us what to do'.[40] The present strategy is top-down, but in the present context the problem of elitism is unimportant. Having a focus, which is what I believe the NJP outline provides, is crucial. The jazz community must work on the detail and see the process through.

My new NJP is influenced by the old plan, in the development of which I was personally involved. Indeed, I have retained some of its wording.[41] The plan needs to address the three areas that bear directly on the health of the Australian jazz scene—

- Career sustainability and audience development
- Jazz infrastructure
- Jazz culture

—and break the vicious cycle of weak economic power and low cultural status that historically has inhibited its development. The issues that divided the jazz community and sank the original plan have evaporated, and at the recent Australia Council-sponsored jazz forum there was wide support for the creation of a new one.

While the NJP would not be totally dependent on public funding, substantial increases in funding levels would play a key role in achieving its goals. The additional funding, annual or triennial, would be channelled through key organizations and project grants to ensembles and individual musicians, to provide increased performance opportunities and substantially increased fees.

The first important step is the creation of a representative national advocacy body that will take on the responsibility to work on the NJP. At the time of writing such a body is being formed.

■

A New National Jazz Plan

Purpose

The NJP seeks to raise the national profile of jazz, increase substantially the national jazz audience and thereby increase all forms of income to jazz and enhance career sustainability for an increasing number of jazz musicians.

Means

It will be necessary for all major jazz organizations and the national advocacy body to accept responsibility for, and work collaboratively on, the detailed development of the NJP in order for it to be implemented successfully. Furthermore, commonwealth and state funding bodies, and existing programs accessed by jazz musicians (Playing Australia, Sound Travellers and CMTP etc.) would be invited to make a commitment to support the plan. `

Key Elements

Properly resourced and well-administered organizations are the key drivers of increased box office, as well as enhanced public and private funding.

- In order that an appropriate response to the needs of the jazz sector as a whole is formulated, it is imperative that funding bodies recognise that low funding levels have obliged jazz organizations to under-resource their administration and maintain a low marketing spend. An increase in financial support is required at the earliest possible opportunity to bolster these areas.

- The increases should target presenting organizations, to enable them to carry out the roles they undertake as part of their commitment to the plan. An increase would also allow these organizations to lift their own non-grant income more effectively.

A national campaign of audience development is central to the NJP. Such a campaign would seek to raise the profile of jazz in the media and offer support to artists/ensembles and private and public presenting organizations. The campaign would operate at regional and national levels and target the electronic, print and virtual media.

- Ideally, and in the first instance, a marketing and pro-motional specialist would develop a feasible strategy for the entire jazz sector, one that is adaptable to meet differing needs. This might be funded through a project grant to one of the presenting organizations.

Crucially, the NJP must address the paucity of adequate venues by calling for the establishment of full-time, dedicated venues in the major centres of Sydney and Melbourne. Elsewhere it may be necessary to establish part-time venues in hotels, theatres or even, perhaps, registered clubs, as appropriate to local conditions.

- Such venues would present innovative programs and involve local groups, groups from outside the region and, where affordable, from overseas. The venues would become centres of energy for the development of jazz and its audience, as well as help sustain a touring circuit. By aggregating income from box office and other trading, they will generate considerably more income to be spent on marketing and promotion, as well as artists' fees.

- The establishment costs of these venues would be sought from the states and, where possible, from local authorities. Capital funding may be necessary for piano, sound and other necessary equipment, while subsidies for the program would be sought from the public and private sectors, and from philanthropic foundations.

The NJP should recognise the important role of individual band leaders as entrepreneurs/presenters and facilitate access to project funding, for example, by scheduling staggered closing-dates and ensuring a quick turn-around time for small grants.

- A small grant program would support activities such as a series of performances in a concert hall, or club; regional and national touring; recording and/or production of a DVD; commissions and contracting of advisory services to practitioners for matters such as marketing and grant applications.

- Such activities would require an immediate injection of funding in order to achieve a significantly greater success rate for applications.

Special support should be directed to emerging artists and a number of large ensembles.

- Emerging artists require support to develop a public profile early in their careers. To this end additional project funding should be provided for rehearsals and performances that are either self-entrepreneured or arranged by an existing presenting organization.
- Additional support for large ensembles would recognise the important role of these groups in encouraging original compositions and arrangements, and in enhancing ensemble-playing skills.

An important element in audience development and the establishment of touring circuits will be the creation of new jazz festivals and the development of existing ones.

- Support should be given for the creation of new jazz festivals in major jazz centres and to well-organized but under-funded regional events. Priority in the allocation of addition funding should be (i) adequate musicians' fees, (ii) an effective level of marketing and promotional spend and (iii) professional administration (including a paid artistic director or a fee to an artistic sub-committee).

For the long-term development of the full spectrum of needs of a viable jazz community (audiences, performers and administrators), education and communication are pivotal.

- Given the strength of tertiary jazz education, support should be provided for projects that target secondary-school students.
- The funding, and viability, of a national jazz magazine should be investigated, or perhaps of a quarterly newspaper, to be distributed free of charge at selected outlets, in the manner of *RealTime*. The possibility of amalgamating such a publication with *RealTime* might be explored.

■

With regard to additional funding, a total of $1.15m over four years should be sought, $400,000 in the first year of the plan, and $250,000 in each of the following three years. The initial figure of $400,000 reflects (approximately) the amount level allocated by the Australia Council to jazz organizations for 2008. The objective is to raise the amount of public funding ultimately allocated to jazz to a total of $2.4m, i.e. double the current amount.

The main thrust of the NJP must be the provision of support for musicians and the development of a larger audience for jazz. As the American critic Gary Giddens puts it, 'Jazz musicians have virtually no access to the machinery of capitalism.'[42] In Australia, at present, they have no more than a small, uncomfortable and precarious seat at the table of subsidised music. They deserve much better.

9

Final thoughts

The Australian contemporary jazz scene is experiencing a period of considerable vitality and, with very limited support, its artists are producing music of surpassing brilliance. However, to secure the music's future there is a need to both reorganize and renew its key support structures and also to find agreement on common goals in order to secure additional funding.

Completing such a program of transformation successfully will present an appreciable challenge to the jazz community. At the national level it will need to demonstrate a unity of purpose and level of co-operation that in the past it has struggled to achieve, while strategies to solve local problems will also have to be devised. For a sector that has tended to be reactive rather than proactive in determining its future course, this will entail considerable planning.

Nevertheless, with a new government in place and a new arts policy to be implemented in Canberra, opportunities will present themselves. The case for increased funding is compelling, not only from the perspective of demonstrated need, but also that of equity in relation to other musical idioms. Jazz has 'made do' with little, but it should not be expected to accept its impoverished condition as a natural and enduring state. The modest improvement in funding suggested here would be an important step towards in liberating jazz from its imprisonment in a permanent underground.

Endnotes

1 'Oehlers tops sax world', *West Australian*, August 2003; 'Local hero has sax appeal', *Australian*, 24 July 2003. The *Australian* did record the fact that there were two other Australian finalists—which is more than any other newspaper or magazine did.

2 John Litweiler, 'Bernie McGann on CD', available at www.sima.org.au/20007/06/11 (accessed 10 February 2008); John Corbett, 'Flying without Ornette', *Chicago Reader*, 29 August 1997.

3 *Observer Music Magazine*, November 2005.

4 If I concentrate here on developments in Sydney and Melbourne, it is partly because of space restrictions and partly because the vast majority of jazz musicians are resident in those two cities The growth and development of contemporary jazz in the other major cities over the last twenty years deserve to be studied in some detail.

5 Why it closed is uncertain, but it is unlikely that it was forced upon it by a decline in patronage.

6 (Kensington: UNSW Press, 1995).

7 The emergence of James Morrison and Vince Jones in the 1980s provided jazz with two very high-profile figures. Morrison, in particular, has become the one jazz musician known to classical, jazz and pop/rock fans everywhere. Although a very successful drawcard, his aesthetic concerns are not those of most young jazz musicians and his music has had little discernable effect on the course of jazz in Australia.

8 The Music Board's Medium-Term Plan, published in 1985, suggested that funding should generally be directed towards 'cutting edge' jazz projects.

9   See Roger Dean on administration in jazz organizations, in *Sounds from the Corner* (Sydney: Australian
Music Centre, 2005), p. 164.

10 Along with Wanderlust, The catholics, Clarion Fracture
Zone, Ten Part Invention, as well as established names
such as Mike Nock, Bernie McGann, Mark Simmonds
and Dale Barlow, all proved consistent drawcards.

11 See <mcakb.wordpress.com/performance/live-perform-
ance/jazz/> (accessed 10 February 2008).

12 A transcript of the forum, 'Jazz 2000 & Beyond', held
on 6 November 2000 is available from the Australia
Council.

13 See George McKay, *Circular Breathing: The Cultural
Politics of Jazz in Britain* (Durham & London: Duke
University Press, 2005), pp. 196ff.

14 See the 'Ad Lib' site, created by Jon Rose on the ABC
web site, at www.abc.net.au (accessed 12 February
2008).

15 Dean, pp. 160, 161.

16 See *Uptown Conversation: The New Jazz Studies*, ed. by
Robert G. O'Meally, Brent Hayes Edwards and Farah
Jasmine Griffin (New York: Columbia University Press,
2004), p. 414. For an interesting discussion of the same
topic, see Yuval Taylor (ed.) *The Future of Jazz* (Chicago:
Acapella Books, 2002), chaps. 4 & 10.

17 *Is Jazz Dead?* (New York: Routledge, 2005), p.120.

18 Dean, p. 168.

19 See his 2006 essay, 'Jazz in Australia', on the 'Music
in Australia Knowledge Base', available at(accessed 10 February 2008).

20 In addition to interviews in Melbourne with Adrian
and Martin Jackson, I relied on my own knowledge
and experience of the Sydney scene and on numerous
informal discussions.

21 NSW Liquor Act 2007. The *State Environmental Planning Policy (Temporary Structures and Places of Public Entertainment 2007)*, which became effective in late October last year, should also facilitate the opening of music venues.

22 The *Report* is available at www.cmc.gov.au/publications (accessed 15 February 2008).

23 'Keith Jarrett Trio, en connivence', *Le Monde*, 30 July 2006.

24 See Graham Strahle, 'Music Criticism in Australia's Major Newspapers', *Music Forum*, January 2008, pp. 42–3. Strahle only considers reviews, not preview pieces or features.

25 This figure does not include recording for ABC Jazz or private hires. Many of these were later released on CD by the artists themselves or through their record companies.

26 www.abc.net.au/tv/set/about.htm

27 A concert by singer Dianne Reeves was the only new jazz offering in the second half of 2007.

28 *The Oxford Companion to Australian Jazz* (Melbourne: OUP, 1987), p. 60. Though 20 years old and badly in need of an up-date, this remains an important book.

29 Arts NSW's funding results for 2008 were not available at the time of writing. I am grateful to the Music Program Officer, Victoria Owens, for confirming that the grants to the organizations in the table would remain unchanged from the 2007 allocations.

30 Machine for Making Sense (MFMS) seeks to generally promote improvised music and interdisciplinary practice. This grant was for Nownow, their bi-monthly concert series.

31 This comparison does not imply criticism of the funding of new music. New music is also under-funded. My point is that, even when measured against a smaller sec-

tor, albeit one with some of the prestige of mainstream classical music, jazz receives considerably less.

32 Personal communication with the author. The figures were also presented at the Australia Council jazz forum held on 14 December 2007.

33 For similar reasons, the grant for improvised music is included in the totals for jazz.

34 I am grateful to Kate Lidbetter for making these figures available to me.

35 MJC received $25,000 from Arts Victoria for 2008.

36 *The Inaudible Music* (Sydney: Currency Press, 2000), pp. 171–2.

37 Excluding the costs of jazz education or ensembles like the West Australian Youth Jazz Orchestra, which I regard as concerned primarily with education.

38 Johnson, p. 172 and Dean, p. 164.

39 See 'Live Work Opportunities', in Bruce Johnson and Shane Homan, *Vanishing acts: an inquiry into the state of live popular music opportunities in New South Wales* (2002), available at www.artsnsw.gov.au/WhatsNew/vanishingacts.htm (accessed 15 February 2008).

40 David Throsby, *Does Australia Need A Cultural Policy?*, Platform Papers No. 7 (Sydney: Currency House, 2006), p. 47.

41 On the jazz scene in north-west Britain, see Kathy Dyson's 2004 report for the Arts Council of England, available at www.artscouncil.org.uk/documents/news/NWJazzdevelopmentreport_phpGYSMvw.pdf_(accessed 18 February 2008).

42 *Weather Bird: Jazz at the Dawn of its Second Century* (Oxford: OUP, 2004), p. 603.

Readers' Forum

Responses to Cathy Hunt and Phyllida Shaw's *A Sustainable Arts Sector: What will it take?*

Richard Letts is the Executive Director of the Music Council of Australia and President of the International Music Council. He has earned a living as a musician and headed a number of non-profit organisations here and in the USA. In a previous century he was Director of the Music Board of the Australia Council.

The recent census shows a quite striking decline from 2001 to 2006 in the number of people declaring their main occupation to be in one of the main art forms: for instance, actors, dancers and related professionals are down by 20%, singers by 25%, instrumentalists by 11%, and visual arts and crafts professionals by 18%. This brings to an end an upward trend of at least four decades duration.[1]

Why is this? It could simply be true that employment in these art forms, whether by self or others, has actually declined. That could be connected to a decline in funding, the effects of technologies, or to a wasting patience with life in the garret.

Or perhaps it reveals not so much a change in occupation as in attitude. What if in the past people gave 'artist' as their main occupation, when actually it was not their primary source of income, but the way in which they wanted to be known? I'm a musician. Oh yeah, I drive a taxi to make some money, but I'm really a musician.

And what if, now, fewer people are identifying themselves as artists, because they think that being an artist has lost its cachet—that society or governments are doubtful about the value of the arts? This is totally speculative, of course.[2]

Cathy Hunt and Phyllida Shaw's *A Sustainable Arts Sector* gives an excellent round-up of strategies by which arts organizations can reconsider and develop their business operations. The authors also recognise that most subsidised arts organizations are flat chat simply keeping their doors open and have neither the time nor the resources to stand back and reconsider their ways of operating. They need respite care, some special one-off assistance to take this step. The recently departed government's reviews of the major performing arts sector and of the orchestras proposed that various survival problems could be ameliorated were the organizations able to build better management. Hunt and Shaw's prescriptions fit comfortably with what already has been government practice here and, as they observe, in Britain.

Of course, arts organizations should operate as efficiently as possible and achieve maximal financial self-reliance. The public purse should not be called upon to prop up poor management.

But what if, after your organization has been McKinseyed and is as taut and 'vibrant' as a violin e-string, you still need subsidy? If you are an orchestra, an opera company, a theatre or dance company putting large numbers on stage, you are an organization with nineteenth-century labour dependency trying to operate in the twenty-first century. Even though you may play to full houses, you cannot cover your costs from box office. If you are a small company presenting high-risk innovative art, you also will not meet your costs from box office, unless you reduce them in the time-honoured fashion by not paying your artists.

So how can we call your operations 'sustainable'? Your management expertise may reduce your trading deficit, but you survive only for as long as the subsidies are there, whether from governments or private sources.

While Hunt and Shaw's sustainability paper is admirable in many ways, it falls in with the *Zeitgeist* in proposing a business solution to what is not, at base, a business problem.

The issue is ultimately about values. At some point in the paper, the authors give a scenario in which government 'cannot' afford to meet arts organizations' increased costs arising from inflation. The proposition is fallacious. In the greater scheme of things, the amount of funds is minute. Of course, a government is *able* to meet those costs. The issue is one of values and resolve.

And this is the case also for the larger funding issues. The difference between a little subsidy and a little less subsidy, a difference that good management can make, will not change the mind of a government that does not believe that arts subsidy delivers a public good—or *enough* public good. The issue is not whether we give attention to being more effective managers—of course, we can and should do that—but that we think that that will resolve the problems of sustainability. It won't. We still have to get funds from government. We can say 'Hey, look, we cleaned up our act. We don't need as much subsidy to survive.' So then we get less subsidy and are still vulnerable. (And what we really needed was a bit more, to bankroll that stuff that you really, *really* can't do from box office, the risky stuff, the larger scale stuff—the things that truly sustainable 'arts' sectors like the pop-music industry, the musical-theatre industry more or less, airport-novel publishers, art auction houses, wouldn't touch with a 40-foot pole.)

As a tactic, we in the arts adopt the language and concepts of those we seek to persuade. Then we slowly fall in with our own propaganda and forget where we came from. Remember the horror when people started referring to the arts as an industry in order to give it an appearance of economic credibility? Now there are probably some younger readers who have never thought of it as anything else.

We do have to find ways to reassert the value of the arts. Art for art's sake. (Well, art for the spirit's sake, and I speak as an atheist.) Somehow, we have accepted that this is a hopelessly fey, indulgent and old-fashioned construct. Well, is it? I would assert that it is much closer to the core than art for the sake of business or the economy. Arguments for the arts as sleek and up-to-the-minute businesses are intrinsically flawed if the businesses are not profitable.

A society in which people claim to be artists even while earning their living as taxi drivers is headed in the right direction.

PS. I acknowledge the excellent arts Future Fund proposal which, however, could benefit from some scenario planning to consider possible effects on other funding.

1   Annotated statistics can be found in the Music in Australia Knowledge Base on the Music Council of Australia website, at www.mca.org.au (accessed 20 February 2008).

2   Setting aside this little riff, those are remarkable figures and demanding of real analysis. What is going on here?

Di Yerbury was CEO of the Australia Council between 1984 and 1986, and Vice-Chancellor of Macquarie University from 1987 until 2006.

Let's put our hands together for those enlightened universities which see it as part of their mission to be arts and cultural centres for both their own communities and for the general public. Cathy Hunt and Phyllida Shaw's title asks *A Sustainable Arts Sector: What will it take?* Well, these universities are already showing how the higher education sector can make its own contribution to the sustainability of the arts.

Both NIDA, the country's first and best-known theatre school, and the Australia Ensemble, one of our finest chamber music groups, are resident at the University of New South Wales, and have been generously nurtured by that university since their foundation in 1963 and 1980 respectively.

Melbourne Theatre Company, the longest established professional theatre company in the country, is actually a department of the University of Melbourne. (Incidentally, there's an added incentive for the university's own staff to swell the audiences: since MTC plays are an in-house product of the university, subscriptions are regarded as an in-house benefit for tax purposes, so staff can elect to pay for them through salary sacrifice, thus discounting the cost of tickets.)

Several campuses are home to performing arts venues: witness Monash's Alexander Theatre, where the Bell Shakespeare Company, amongst others, tours regularly, and its Robert Blackwood Concert Hall, which seats 1600 and can accommodate a full symphony orchestra. Brisbane's professional arts venues include the Queensland University of Technology's cultural precinct, with its popular Gardens Theatre.

The Perth International Festival, the oldest international festival of its kind in the southern hemisphere, was founded at the University of Western Australia in 1953; and, as part of that Festival, both UWA and Edith Cowan University host the outdoor LotteryWest Festival Films program. ECU does so in a lakeside setting on its picturesque Joondalup Pines campus, with free BBQ facilities for families. The screens also light up under the stars at UWA's Somerville Auditorium.

Partnerships between arts organizations and educational institutions can take many forms. Starting with the support of the Australia Council's first Partnership Grant, the coupling of the creative talents of Kim Carpenter's Theatre of Image with Macquarie University's technological capacity, made possible the innovative multi-media component of many ToI productions between 1996 and 2005, including two which won Helpmann Awards for Best Presentation for Children.

The two national *Cinderella Collections* reports in the 1990s highlighted the value of university museums and collections to Australia's distributed movable heritage. By far the most numerous in terms of category (and generally the best cared-for), are the art collections and galleries. A lot of such campus-based galleries and museums welcome school groups with guided tours and age-appropriate educational kits. Some (like Macquarie University's) collaborate with regional and other galleries to tour special exhibitions or lend artworks. And coming back to the University of Melbourne: not only does it host splendid art exhibitions, but also the unique Grainger Museum, with its copious evidence of the creative life of the celebrated composer-pianist.

Over the decades, many sculptors have found it difficult to find not only patrons but also appropriate public spaces in which to exhibit their works. In 1992, sculptor

Errol Davis proposed an imaginative solution in Sydney's northern suburbs, when he craftily congratulated me on hosting Australia's best sculpture park on Macquarie's spacious, leafy campus. Perplexed, I asked: 'But where are all the sculptures?' He swiftly responded: 'Now that's where we come in ...'

The result, with Errol as Curator, is now indeed Australia's leading Sculpture Park and a glorious environment which has encouraged other vice-chancellors to consider similar approaches. In recent years, the University of Western Sydney's arts calendar has included the annual UWS Acquisitive Sculpture Award and Exhibition, with major works by significant Australian artists displayed in the lovely lakeside setting of the Campbelltown campus.

Regional universities play a particularly vital role in their local communities. But they can't do it all on their own. The University of Southern Queensland collaborates with far-sighted community and corporate stakeholders to enhance the region's cultural, creative and artistic life with a range of lively activities and events for all ages. USQ Artworx's annual offerings include the Shakespeare in the Park Festival, the West-Star Motors Twilight Series, the Breez Finance Children's Festival, the Ergon Energy USQ Big Band, an Opera Season and the Summer and Winter Arts Retreats.

What a contribution all these tertiary institutions are making! It's one to which this arts lover responds with warm applause. Long may such benefaction continue, however straitened the times in which the higher-education sector lives!

Nick Hill teaches Arts Management & Media and Communications in the School of Culture and Communications at the University of Melbourne.

First, I want to congratulate Cathy Hunt and Phyllida Shaw on an excellent think piece. The thoughtfulness and nuance of their essay is laudable and their interrogation provokes valid reflection on the artist's role at the very centre of the 'arts ecology'. At the recent Malthouse Theatre launch of the essay an issue that was raised which I think worthy of further consideration. Dance critic Hilary Crampton's metaphor of the arts operating as an 'ecological system'—the metaphor is, in fact, now in widespread use[1]—may be simply but usefully extended to recognise that for ecologies to survive something needs to die; the regeneration is a product of decay.

This must and should be the case with the arts: some organizations, some art, indeed some artists, may simply wander off into the twilight; others should be ushered more speedily from the stage; controversially, perhaps some of the monoliths of culture should be abandoned to the vagaries of the free market. Seemingly this would allow for nascent talent to access the light flowing through the canopy. Even if they too fail, they will at least have been given the *opportunity* to bloom, pollinate and produce works of a high order. Currently, a degree of stasis prevails, often bolstered by rampant managerialism in some of the more established companies—but it is not only at the door of the arts sector that blame for this can be laid. In the current climate of arts funding as it obtains in Australia, there is much to suggest that opportunities to address these problems are being willingly taken up.

Let me turn to a related issue, the practice of tacitly adopting the nomenclature of climate change, the word 'sustainability'. I'm as guilty as anyone of applying 'sustainability' to the arts. But now might be the time to stop, for I'm not sure it's any longer helpful to slip around on the coat tails of the environmentalists. Although Jon Hawkes' 'fourth-pillar' argument is strong, in my recent experience the arts—indeed, culture generally—are still treated as a poor cousin in the wider discussions of sustainability, effectively below the salt as far as the policy makers are concerned.[2] The bailiwick of the climate change advocates is well established and has already been integrated into the corporate codicils without, sadly, much more than a cursory glance towards the arts.

In the arts environment, however, there is an un-limited stock of creativity, unlike the black gold of the fossil fuels or the failures indicated by the darker arts of the economic rationalist. One would hope that art and creative practice might flourish in a climate of risk and difficulty, as has so often been the case with the arts in times of adversity. Thus, the idea of 'arts sustainability', an expression so overwrought now as to have become almost meaningless, might be replaced with imagery of sustenance and support. Hunt and Shaw's argument needs to recognise that arts organizations must present a clearly defined and occasionally radical profile, rather than hope to benefit vicariously from whatever crumbs might fall from the sustainability table.

I have argued elsewhere that the support and vitality of the arts is at heart an issue of patronage. This refers not simply to the mechanical largesse of funding bodies, often coupled with an awkward, implicit subservience, but also points to the fact that the arts are a positive result of the extended patronage environment from which they emerge and to which they still very much belong. Thus, patronage might include, for instance, the educational opportunities available to the artist; the choices audiences (and critics) may make; the style, taste and enthusiasm of publics, and the very visceral needs of communities—let alone those of the public/private mix of philanthropists, arts bureaucracies or corporate sponsors. In a gentler sense, this points to the wider aegis under which the arts might flourish.

Thus, although the extremely complicated model that incorporates patronage has multiple strands of influence and effect, it nevertheless positions the artist or arts experience, as Hunt and Shaw emphasise, firmly at the very centre of what will always be a labyrinthine debate. Whether this results in a Future Fund for the Arts remains to be seen, but having a language that negotiates the new working practices of arts organizations in relation to their funders will go some way to ensuring a vital and dynamic future for the arts sector.

1   See Keith Gallasch's *Art in a Cold Climate: Rethinking the Australia Council*, Platform Papers No. 6 (Sydney: Currency House, 2004).

2   See Hawkes' *Fourth Pillar of Sustainability: Culture's Essential Role in Public Planning* (Melbourne: Cultural Development Network & Common Ground, 2001).

Subscribe to **Platform Papers**

Have the papers delivered quarterly to your door

4 issues for $55.00 including postage within Australia

The individual recommended retail price is $13.95.

___ I would like to subscribe to 4 issues of Platform Papers for $55.00

I would like my subscription to start from: ___ this issue (No. 16)

___ the next issue (No. 17)

Name_____

Address_____

_____

_____ State _____ Postcode _____

Email _____

Telephone _____

Please make cheques payable to Currency House Inc.

Or charge: ___ Mastercard ___ Visa

Card no. ___ ___ ___ ___ ___ ___ ___ ___ ___ ___ ___ ___

___ ___ ___ ___

Expiry date _____ Signature _____

Fax this form to Currency House Inc. at: 02 9319 3649

Or post to: Currency House Inc., PO Box 2270, Strawberry Hills NSW 2012 Australia

CURRENCY HOUSE